PILLAR # 2

"The Finance"

TO SUSTAIN A HEALTHY AND STABLE RELATIONSHIP

RUBEN B. HEADLEY

GRISELDA DE HEADLEY

COPYRIGHT

Dedication

I dedicate this series exclusively to couples who try to preserve their relationships, and seek the means to achieve this goal. I hope that it will be of great help to those concerned and achieve the objectives for which they acquired this book.

Heading

"Start the Root of the evil tree today; And tomorrow you will not have the misery to eat its fruits."

"Everything that man sows that will minds."

"Law of Cause and Effect."

Prologue

This book was written so that millions of couples can learn to build the 3 Pillars that support a Healthy and Stable relationship. Whoever follows this manual may become an excellent teacher, counselor, and partner.

The experiences you will be able to acquire in this series is the compilation of years of counseling instructed to the couples who wanted to strengthen their relationships.

I invite you to enjoy every page of this book.

Contenido

"BEING A PERFECT COUPLE DOESN'T MEAN NO PROBLEM. BUT KNOW TO OVERCOME IT TOGETHER."

This series is to be an integral part of the first book already published in the series, the **3 Pillars to Sustain a Healthy and Stable** Relationship, No.**1 "Communication".**" If you haven't read it, I invite you to do it, so you have a sequence in the whole series.

Likewise, this book has the purpose, of taking you in a different, practical and simple way, to solve complex situations that manifest themselves in the relationship because of finance, will help you make the most accurate decisions when you need to make it.

Undoubtedly this book will expand your mind and clarify your vision of bringing finance into a home, which is one of the 3 essential pillars to sustain a Healthy Relationship.

Imagine well balanced and balanced Relationship, after knowing how to build the 3 Pillars that support a Healthy Relationship!

INTRODUCTION

First of all, I would like to start with several questions.

Should Woman? Can you work to support the home or the relationship.?

The Man Must? Or can you? Work to support the home or relationship?

In these modern times, we have seen such scenarios in the relationship, where the money that enters is no longer enough to support a family or a home, and it is where the woman makes the decision to work, and together with her partner to face the commitments.

If we travel back in time with our menthe, and go a little towards the times of our ancestors, whether in the early period, medieval times, or simply a century ago, we will be able to observe that the responsibility of provision has always fallen upon Man.

While it is true even in sacred scripture God places man's responsibility in the garden, giving him the order that he should work, and even when God disobeys that with the sweat of his forehead Man would eat from bread.

I hope you have answered the two initial questions correctly, just as in this book you will be able to answer them once you finish reading it. At your own discretion.

"Money is not enough when the need grows", but if it grows luxuries is not called necessity, it is called Capriccios."

"Being rich is not the one who has the most but the one who needs the least"

"Cover yourself as far as your blanket reached, if you want to cover your feet more, then lengthen your blanket"

Don't spend your money, let alone things that aren't necessary, just to show people that you can have it or to make people believe that you're well financially. "It Should be like throwing your money in a broken bag, you'll never see it again.

As in the first series delivered, real-life cases will also be exposed, where you can surely identify with one of them, and take appropriate measures to avoid any kind of situations that want to arise.

Remember that the key to avoid all the origins of the problem remains the same:

"Start from Root, to the bad tree today; so, you don't have the misery to eat its fruits tomorrow"

Chapter 1

Building El Pilar #2 to sustain a Healthy and Stable Relationship

FINANCE

To understand this topic, it is necessary to understand that finance has a lot of definition, depending on the area you want to deal with, whether in a company, in a business, in a company, etc., but this is not the case. We'll talk about finances within the relationship, but we won't teach math, accounting or anything like that, what we're going to learn is the art of solving the problems caused by finance within the home, whether there was abundance, or scarcity of it within the relationship.

In my first book, where we talk about the Pillar #1 which is "The Communication", we manage to see that this pillar for it to be effective in the relationship, depends fully on the couples and their maturity.

Instead, this Pillar #2 "Finance" is fully dependent on the Pillar #1, so that it can be effective in the relationship.

Although it may seem unreal, when there is abundance within a relationship, it, makes no guarantee that a healthy and much less stable relationship can be sustained, whether for the reason it arises, it does not escape the reasons for discussions at home.

Instead, if there is a shortage, it is likely that the relationship may be going through a moment of stress and therefore discussion.

Now imagine achieving a perfect balance with your partner, whether having plenty or scarcity in your relationship.

Without a doubt, you have often wondered how a relationship can look more stable than yours, having more resources than they do.

You may also have noticed that there are relationships that have better economic facilities than yours, but their lives lack satisfaction or happiness. It happens in the movies, they happen in the Novels, but it also happens in real life, very close to us.

The answer is simple and simple: **"They have not been able to efficiently build the 3 Pillars that support a Healthy and Stable Relationship"**

Elements that integrate a Healthy and Stable Finance into the relationship

Just as we work with the elements in the first book: Pillar #1 "Communication", it is essential that we also take into account that, in order to have a Healthy and Stable Finance in Relationship, it is important to know some of the elements that make up it, I have taken three of the most important things that we must ensure that they are not lacking:

Communication:

It will always be an important factor in all Pillars. It is the main basis of the Triangle that forms finance in the relationship.

In the first book we know extensively all the details of this element, we know what its enemies are (Cezanne).

Planning:

Without well-organized and disciplined planning, it would be impossible to achieve a healthy and stable finance, so it is important to sit with the couple and use verbal communication, to organize the expenses incurred throughout the relationship.

Your enemy or Tares: Disorganization, and Lack of Communication.

Knowledge:

One of the keys to carrying a Healthy and Stable Finance in Relationship, is precisely the knowledge of what you want to obtain. It is nourished by the information that is acquired to have a clearer and more extensive picture when acting with income and outflows in the relationship. It is also important to know the feelings and concepts about your proceeding when acquiring a possession and attitude towards your partner.

Your enemy or Tares: Disinformation and Apathy.

Apathy: A state of selflessness and lack of motivation or enthusiasm in which a person finds himself and that involves indifference to any extreme stimulus.

CHAPTER 2

Meaning of finance

As I said in the previous chapter, when we talk about finance, it depends on what area we are going to apply knowledge, whether in a company, in a business, in a company, but in this case, we will talk about the definition of personal finance in the relationship.

For me before proceeding, it is essential to be able to offer some details and tools, so that they have it as their basis, either in the present if they are not carrying it out, or in the future where you need guidance on the subject. This book will be an essential tool as part of your financial life. Following these concepts can lead you to a simpler and more comfortable way of life in your personal relationship.

All the tips you will receive through this book, maybe you don't need it today, or you don't understand it now, but you'll definitely use it later.

Personal Finance:

Personal finances are where heads of families or the couple as a whole manage resources throughout the relationship. In this case we may include, not only the income and expenses received or paid during the relationship, but also the form, tools or financial products that in the relationship manage to acquire, to optimize the management of their resources, to achieve a common objective

CHAPTER 3

<u>SET OBJECTIVES</u>

This personal finance teaching aims to help individuals and families make **"informed"** decisions, **which** allow to optimize the management of their resources. It is very important, when **we** are **in a** relationship, manages **to** communicate, se, **in order to achieve a series of joint and** priority objectives as I will mention in the following lines.

Protection:
have a certain amount of untouchable money, for adequate protection from risks or unforeseen events.

A responsible couple should set out to have an emergency fund, and have the discipline not to touch it, forget that it exists and try to maintain a positive balance, **so as** not to have the need to incur it.

Emergency funds:
As the word describes it, it is used only for emergency types that the couple agrees to, for

which it will be used at the time it is presented to them. An example of these would be: medical expenses, unexpected dismissals, car damage, etc.

INFORMED DECISIONS

When we talk about **"Informed"** decisions, ", we commonly refer to the partner's orientation **de in** investing their money, i.e. raising awareness towards the purchase of assets that generate short- and long-term well-being in the relationship, and not liabilities that generate short- medium- and long-term expenses.

In summary: The writer Robert Kiyosaki defines these two concepts in a very simple way:

Assets: It's all that puts money into your pocket. (Also known as Income or Money Entries)

Liabilities: It's everything that takes money out of your pocket. (Also known as Egress or money out)

Depending on the purpose or purpose for which something was acquired.

(Example: buying a house or a car can become a liability, if it is only used as luxury or necessity, because that way they will both demand expenses on energy and fuel and letter payments.

But they become assets if both are used to generate income, i.e. rental of the house, or use the vehicle as a form of transport to generate income, either through a platform, taxi or haulage, etc.)

To manage to keep a good control in the personal finance in the relationship, it is important that the couple sit down and establish a Plan to establish their spending priorities, and not change their goal.

"If the Plan doesn't work, then the ideal is to change the Plan and not the goals."

Why do I mean this? There's a great phrase I like to repeat.

"People spend money they don't have, on things they don't need, to make an impression on people they don't even care about."

Investment:
It is to accumulate or get enough cash, by buying assets, which will positively influence the quality of life that is desired. Once you make an investment, then the next step is to use the profits to acquire a desired good. So, for example, pay a career at the university (without worrying about monthly payment, no annual payment, buying a car without having to keep paying for lyrics, likewise a house, or starting your own business, etc.)

Personally, at the beginning of my relationship I did not know the importance of these concepts, and the need to put them into practice. I remember that a few years ago, at a time when the economy of the country was very stable, we had the necessary resources to try to make an environment change, as far as social status of life is concerned, we had the intention of going to move to a very exclusive residential of our city, where there was ample and spacious housing at a good price for us, it was a closed complex with pool and social area, that our children could enjoy very well. We had already spoken to the bank; it was just to give the initial credit to make it ours.

We said it was time to change our life status, and personally I wanted to do as I said in the phrase above, "Spending the money I didn't have, on things I didn't need at the time, to impress people I don't know." I wanted them to know that we were moving to another standard of living. It is a very common mistake that is repeated in people who come from a very low social status, I think it is about self-esteem.

Well, we lived in an undeveloped slum. Our financial entry allowed us to do it without any problem, but something happened along the way, things didn't start to go well, started a line of problems in the company where I still own it to today, but the finances in that moment began to wane and we had to give up on the idea of moving to an exclusive residential.

Later, about Approx. 5 years later, I began to know these principles that I present to you in this Book. Hoy day we have 3 houses of our own, in different part of the country, the house where we started our relationship, and we raise our children, we also have a cottage, and one that we are building that by the end of this year we will move in, and will be the Principal with which I will live with the family, will have its pool and social area, and best of all that we are building to our liking. Tiene two levels, in each level there are 225 m2, without duty any money to any bank, we have own car canceled in full, and always the opportunity to cancel the school year of our children. In this book you will see the tips and learn from the teachings that will leave the stories we will see later. Although it takes us a while to put it into practice, once we knew this concept, we no longer make hasty decisions, we simply live according to the opportunity presented to us. As soon as we need to make an expense, we first sit-down, talk and analyze the good, the bad and the ugly of what will be the decision we make, after doing that exercise, we are ready to decide. This way of doing things has helped us to sustain a Healthy and Stable relationship, thanks to "**Communication**" **and** how we are carrying "**Finance**".

But before we got to this balance point, my wife and I had a lot of trouble saving, every time we tried in the long run we would consume what we had saved, then we sat down to discuss what we were doing wrong, or that it prevented us from achieving our savings goals. And conclude the following:

"The higher debt and lower income, the less the ability to save." In other words, the first thing we decided to do was write off the ant debts and expenses.

Ant expenses are those that do not sit, nor are not noticed, but that produced outflows of money every fortnight, for example: Informal loans, as bi-weekly lenders, we reduced night outs, also expenses in restaurants, we dedicate the car to the financial, to avoid that monthly exit, reduce the passage through the highway toll , even reducing expenses at birthday parties.

All of this we did as part of the sacrifice that we had to acquire a Healthy finance and manage to save without having to touch the saved again, added to that, we increase our economic entry, through online businesses, which to date leave us good dividends.

Once you become familiar with this step, it is expendable to fulfill the following commitments:

Tax Compliance:
it is important to always have the resources to pay on time the taxes and other expenses required by law, so that interest, payments, or bank commitments you have at the time to avoid extraordinary payments, or interest rates, are not accumulated later.

Planning an early retirement.

Retirement:
It is important to recognize that the years will pass and the forces will run out, and he who did not make corrections in time will have to work to eat and not eat for work.

If you have enough daring to start a business, and make it profitable. (in my book "Healthy Business Profitability"), you can follow a more detailed guide to start your own profitable business and secure cash flow while you're alive.

Liquidity:
Having the quality of keeping cash in your wallet is a good habit, as long as you're not teaching it everywhere **to provoke the owners of** others. I'm just trying to carry no more than 500 cash with me, if I'm going to go out with the family and not more than 200 if I'm just in the everyday.

Planning:
define a strategy on how objectives can be carried out and what are the appropriate financial instruments.

Monitoring and re-evaluation:
monitor plan compliance, check for relevant changes in initial conditions, and assess whether an adjustment or change in the financial plan is necessary.

CHAPTER 4

Case objectives

The different cases that we are going to deal with, aim to be a reflection of the situations in each couple. And it is true that we cannot cover all the many situations that may exist in relationships, but I will take as a reference some of the most prominent cases that I have had to attend to.

Hoping to help millions of couples around the world, it's what motivates me to write this book. That it manages to be an instrument that passes from generation to generation and that can be established in each couple, a Healthy and Stable Relationship.

May each Couple overcome the adversities presented by these cases and gain greater knowledge in the subject.

That they can live together wisely and peacefully in marriage. Did you know that marriage is the first institution established directly by God?

Case Analysis Dynamics

Now you can re-analyze   each case, using the Question Guide, which were used in the first series of this Book "The Communication" established in case 1 of Brayan and Melanie. What conclusions would you draw from these problems.? If you have not yet read the book, I invite you to pause, get it borrowed with a friend or download it directly from the Amazon www.amazon.com/author/rubenheadleystore, will help you know how to solve these topics, and you will know the dynamics applied in them.

 For your own conclusions according to your criteria, once you have answered each of the questions, you will be able to compare your answer from question Number 10, at the end of the page with the case number. The main one we need to know, is where the whole problem that caused it originated, and how it could have been avoided, so that this situation would not become a problem in the relationship. (This question series will serve all the cases presented here).

1. Locate the place where the problem originated.

2. Determine what type of Communication was used before the Conflict?

3. Analyze the first mistake made by one of the two.

4. Define who misinform understanding the Communication sent.

5. Discuss what the couple tried to communicate at that time.

6. At what point the Tares was planted.

7. Which Pillar Element was affected and which tares was sown on the other side?

8. What action or actions do you think bothered the other party?

9. Identify how many types of pillar elements have been affected and which types of tares have been sown in this conflict." Explain it."

10. What was the real origin that caused the whole problem and how could it be avoided.? (Resolving this Question will be the primary key to avoid any Conflict in the future).

"The evil tree starts today from its root; so that tomorrow you don't have the misery to eat its fruits."

CHAPTER 5

Case #1

Laura and Fernando

Who is responsible for home finances?

In the introduction I asked 2 question:

Should Woman? Can you work to support the home or the relationship.?

The Man Must? Can you work to support the home or the relationship.?

There has always been a controversy over the duties and rights of men and women in a relationship, many have a proper concept, but in the same way many have it wrong. My question is: Why does the man decide to take the woman from her comfort, then not take responsibility for her?"

Laura and Fernando came to my office one afternoon, because they had a very serious problem every day that It was Laura's turn to receive payment of her salary, because she refused to leave half her money in the expenses of the house, but Fernando stressed that she should help with the expenses of the household because she works , and also lives under the same roof, so it was his duty to help.

She said; she had no problem "contributing" to expenses, but what she didn't think was right was feeling compelled to pay for home expenses. Because if so, what was the use of having a husband.

Did I ask Fernando, what did he think about the duties and right of women in the home?

He answered me and said, "Well! I have always seen that when a woman works it is to help the husband with household expenses, because we both share the same roof.

I asked him, if the two had ever sat down to talk about what home expenses would be like, and what would his obligation be like? In what he said by saying, we didn't think it necessary to talk because that was an obvious issue, he's not the only one who works and pays the expenses, the women of my friends do it and they don't resist, or complain like Laura.

Then I asked him the following:

When they didn't live together yet, and you asked her out, who paid the exit expenses? He said: I

Why didn't you let her pay the expenses? Because I was the one who invited her, Fernando replied.

Okay, you know, if you gave her the condition that she paid for everything, possibly today they wouldn't be together, because she'd already be warned of the kind of man you are, and I can assure you 90% that maybe she wouldn't have made the decision to join you. (In my book, "qualities a woman seeks in a man") this topic explains this topic in more detail.

Every woman joins a man, because the impression she gave them is that he would take care of her, not her with him, financially speaking.

"The woman joins the man to feel that someone protects, cares for her and provides him, not the other way around"

The answer to the question: Should a woman or can she work to sustain household expenses? it is as follows:

Every woman when she decides to join a man, is because one of the qualities she found in him, was what he would be his supplier, unless before they got married, they had talked about what coexistence would be like under the same roof. Then man could question her for not fulfilling the part of his covenant.

But in the first instance the woman is not "MUST" be obliged to work to pay for the expenses of the house, but if "CAN" help with expenses if she wishes. When a woman works, often a man must let her do so that she can feel useful, and can have her own income and not rely on a man to pay her for the beauty salon, shoes, makeup etc. (although she also enters the role of the man suffering from his personal needs).

Instead, a man does not "CAN", he yes "MUST" by obligation to work and see how he sustains household expenses, it is not an option, it is his responsibility as "Alpha Male" to do. If you don't feel able to carry that burden, then you should have thought about it before you joined.

Many men today prefer to live alone, precisely for this reason, who do not want to feel pressured by the need that comes with a home, for them it is easier to live alone and that no one depends on Him.

In the event that the relationship has Good communication, and Man Will be come without a fixed entry, it is where the duty of women to support the costs that come at home comes in, because it is the right aid.

But what if the woman doesn't work, and the man will be out of a job?

These are the difficult times that arise in couples, not to separate from each other, but to join more, create plans and strategies to get ahead.

"The Diamonds, comes out of the carbon grace at the pressure exerted by the atmosphere."

"Make your dark moments like charcoal, a precious Diamond come out."

"He who is unwilling to risk more than normal shall settle for the ordinary."

CASE ANALYSIS #1

1. Locate the place where the problem originated.

A- The Problem originated at the couple's house.

Tip: Apparently this problem was happening a long time ago, so in many relationships it happens until there comes a time when the discomfort manifests and is where couples should seek help if in that case, they cannot solve it on their own.

2. Determine what type of Communication was used before the Conflict?

A- Open communication was used verbally, from both.

Tip: If you do not know the types of communication you can find it in the first series the Pillar #1 communication.

3. Analyze the first mistake made by one of the two.

A- The first mistake made was by Fernando, as he intended by means of an adulation to force Laura to leave half her salary, when she had never talked about such treatment.

Tip: In every relationship there must be good communication about home finance, what each person's duties and rights will be.

4. Define who lacked the Communication sent.

A- Fernando lacks to understand the verbal communication issued for Laura, not to be comfortable with the proposal he was offering her.

Tip: Important to understand the communication sent by the couple, analyze their views and try to be as equitable as possible, a happy couple certainly guarantees a healthy relationship.

5. Discuss what the couple tried to communicate to them at that time.

R- Laura informed Fernando, that it was not fair for him to have the intention that she should contribute 50% of the expenses of the house.

Tip: Suddenly they'll think Fernando wasn't asking

Laura for anything strange, but actually what he was proposing to his wife doesn't go according to the principles of a home. Man must always be the one who provides providence, security, and trust to the home. Changing this format can cause distortion in the relationship and later a series of situations will be created in which it will be to regret.

6. At what point the Tares was planted.

A- The tares were sown at the time they decided to join and not organize, let alone the duties and rights of each.

Tip: Important! Always talk about each other's finances, duties and rights.

7. Which Pillar Element was affected and which tares was sown on the other side?

A- The element of the affected pillar in the other part was Planning, since one of its main enemies or tares is the lack of communication, in terms of expenses and finance.

Tip: Without Planning you can't get far, because you can't there is a clear goal, let alone a goal, by which they can be directed to achieve it.

"Tell me what your plan is and I'll tell you how far you can go"

8. What action or actions do you think bothered the other party?

R- Laura was annoyed by the obligatory way Fernando demanded to contribute at home.

Tip: When you want to get something from your partner, you need to become wise with words, tone of voice, and intent of it.

9. Identify how many types of pillar elements have been affected and which types of tares have been sown in this conflict." Explain it."

A- The Pillars Affected in this Relationship were: Communication, which brought with its selfishness, and the planning that brought with its disorganization in the plans.

10. What was the real origin that caused the whole problem and how could it be avoided.? (Resolving this Question will be the primary key to avoid any Conflict in the future).

"The evil tree begins today from its root; so that tomorrow you will not have the misery to eat of its fruits."

CHAPTER 6

Case #2
Francisco y Paula

A Hidden Beauty

Why owe spend our money on things that don't satiate, or produce, ignoring investment in more efficient issues?

I have discovered that a man before a relationship, always promises to be an attentive, responsible, kind and caring person, in fact, it is what every woman thinks before joining a man, but once married or attained the goal, the man forgets his principles and becomes an egocentric being, forgetting or setting aside the woman who decided to enter into that uncertain adventure.

Francisco and Paula live in a residential, what is considered lower middle class, the wife of Francisco, always looked sad and shy with people, but Francisco seemed to be a strong character and who always has everything under control, he likes to be the center of attraction with friends, so his life must be exemplary. He works in an office getting a good salary, he was a person who, when he walked past a store, and something caught his eye, he didn't hesitate to buy it. His home had all the technology that went out of fashion, 50" flat screen, sound equipment, theater at

66

home, the car he had invested more than 5 thousand dollars in sound equipment, screens, etc. Francis really didn't lack anything, all he was bothering was to get home and see his wife always lined up, her hair tied up, and her dress to be at home. Every time he saw her like this, he reproached her for her appearance.

Paula was a very beautiful woman when Francisco met her, she always tried to look good and fashionable, she was always makeup and combed, but after a while, exactly 2 years, since she decided to move in with Francisco, she stopped taking care of herself, and although Paula is still beautiful, her appearance does not show the beauty that is in her.

One day I went to his house and was fascinated by everything he had in his home, he liked to show off his possessions. At that moment the Paula comes out to bring me a glass of juice, on a facade that did not like to see Francisco. When he saw her, he did not hesitate to humiliate her in front of me by telling her; you are not ashamed or with the visit to go out on that facade, you better have stayed locked in the room as you always do when there are visitors.

Paula sad, ashamed and with tears-filled eyes sat weeping, saying she could no longer stand for that humiliation on Francis' part, I no longer want to be with him.

I immediately intervened in that problem to know the root of the couple's bitterness.

I told you to talk! Let's see Francisco, because you treat Paula like that in front of me, which is what really bothers you.

Francis said: Look! what happens is that when I met her, I fell in love because she always tried to look good, there was no day when she did not take care of her appearance, I always saw her with her hair arranged, her pretty Clothes, her nails painted, always made up and her aroma was delicious for the perfumes that she placed. But now I don't know where that Paula I met got in,every time I arrive, just to see her fill me with anger, because of her lack of care since we live together, I envy my friends because their women are always well groomed to receive the visits, You yourself have seen how she received it. I'm sick of this too!

I told Paula to calm down and have a glass of water so she could talk.

Paula said: Look! It's true everything Francis says, two years ago that I came to live with him, and really after a while I stopped getting my hair done and put attention to my appearance, but when he proposed me to come and live with him, before that I worked, he had my own income, he for his jealousy told me to leave the job that he would take care of my expenses. So far, he has been very responsible with the expenses of the house, the light, the food, but what he has not understood, that the woman he is looking for is still in here, the only inconvenience that woman has no means to take her out again. He never gives me money for me to fix me, go through a beauty salon, or go out to buy clothes, I think Francis thinks that with paying the expenses of the house and bringing the food is enough, he always claims my appearance, but he keeps bringing expensive artifact to the house, the prettier the house that I see , because he's just here to show off, but he doesn't realize that I also need to feel good about myself. I don't ask him for money, because the time I tried to tell him, to give me some cash, he told me that if I was blind and didn't see that he's just carrying the house expenses, and that he didn't have the money to give me. From that day on, I promised myself that I would never ask him for money again, so that he would never humiliate me again, but he has not yet stopped. And I Reilly can't take it anymore.

Then I looked at Francis and he just lowered his head, feeling ashamed, because of how self-centered he had been and had not realized that the only one responsible for Paula's bad appearance was him.

From that day things changed between them, they did not separate, because Francis asked Paula for forgiveness, and recognized that it had been he who had been making the mistake for two years, today he has the Paula he met, now he no longer spends alone on him, now Paula became part of his priority.

"Many times, we fall into the mistake of Losing the Moon, for looking at the stars"

"When you find a person, who cares for you, listens to you, encourages you, then you have found one more reason to say: I love you"

THE WOMAN YOU WANT ISN'T GONE; SHE'S LOCKED IN HERSELF, GET HER OUT OF THERE AND YOU'LL FIND IN YOUR HOUSE WHAT YOU'VE BEEN LOOKING FOR OUTSIDE!

CASE ANALYSIS #2

1. Locate the place where the problem originated.

A- The problem of this case originated in the heart of Francis.

Tip: When a person becomes self-centered and forgets the need his partner has, it is because his heart has been filled with vanity and selfishness.

2. Determine what type of Communication was used before the Conflict?

A- The communication that was used by Paula was verbally open.

Tip: The need for a couple must be a priority in the relationship, and in the background the vanities that attract us to acquire it, following this advice you can build a relationship, healthy and stable.

3. Analyze the first mistake made by one of the two.

A- The first mistake was made by Francis, when he created an intimidation of Paula when she wanted to ask him for money to settle down, and secondly for losing his wife's priority.

Tip: Never miss the main goal when you decide to join and go live together with the couple.

4. Define who lacked the Communication sent.

R- Francisco failed to understand the communication sent by Paula.

Tip: Every couple always has a peculiar way to communicate a request to their partner, often they will hesitate to ask the couple something, depending on the character and temperament of the other party.

5. Discuss what the couple tried to communicate to them at that time.

R- Paula tried to tell Francisco, that she would like to have some money, for her own expenses.

Tip: A man must understand that a woman not only lives on what he can supply her to eat, but she also requires a small freedom to give herself some personal darlings. The heaviest job is being a housewife, and often you work without compensation. A housewife, works 24 hours a day, 7 days a week, and 365 days a year, since her profession is multipurpose, she must be a cook, a washer, a nanny, often a nurse, other times a doctor, teacher, plumber, receptionist etc. Don't you think a housewife doesn't deserve a salary?

6. At what point the Tares was planted.

A- At the moment Francis decides to dismiss Paula in his priorities, in which he was sown the tares of selfishness.

Tip: Many people are dominated by vanity, the need for acceptance and wanting to feel superior to others or worse still trying to be someone who really isn't, makes you forget what really matters in a relationship.

7. Which Pillar Element was affected and which tares was sown on the other side?

A- The main element that was affected was the

Communication, leading to the shearing of selfishness being sown in Francis.

Tip: It is everyone's duty to pay attention to their partner's words and never to belittle their thoughts or their word.

8. What action or actions do you think bothered the other party?

A- Paula was annoyed by Francisco's attitude when he asked him for money for his personal expenses, and to see that he spent more on vanities than on her.

Tip: If your partner isn't happy about what you spend your money on, then your investment is in a broken bag. Many times, we spend on Passive (Everything that takes money out of your pocket), but never active (Any investment that deposits money in your pocket).

9. Identify how many types of pillar elements have been affected and which types of tares have been sown in this conflict." Explain it."

A- The elements of the pillar affected in this

relationship were communication, and The Knowledge of not knowing how to invest the money, brought with it the tares of Misinformation and Apathy in Francis.

Tip: It is necessary that, in order to have a healthy and stable relationship, they have a good knowledge in the area of finance, because for lack of information large mistakes are made falling into unpayable debts, once you fall into that hole, you cannot go out so easily. Before you spend your money on something, stop and think, if you really need to buy that, or it was just a part of you that drives you to buy it.

10. What was the real origin that caused the whole problem and how could it be avoided.? (Resolving this Question will be the primary key to avoid any Conflict in the future).

"The evil tree begins today from its root; so that tomorrow you don't have the misery to eat its fruits"

CHAPTER 7
#3 CASE
Yolanda and Ricardo
Character Change

"People will notice the changes in our attitude towards them, but they will never notice the behavior of theirs that made us change."."

A few years ago, I had a friend comforted, his name is Ricardo, even though he lived with his wife, he had practically lost her. It was like that saying, "TOGETHER, BUT NOT SCRAMBLED." He started the conversation in a very sad voice and said: I think I'm going to separate myself from Yolanda. And why do you want to do it? I asked him.

For she is no longer the Yolanda that we both met, she is not that housewife dedicated to her home, dedicated to her family, she now has a job and there is no day that does not arrive smell of alcohol and very late at night, I no longer discuss anything, because every time I do she comes bitter and insults me , tells me that it is none of my business what she does with her life, that I am good at nothing she tells me.

Actually, I no longer want to live like that with Yolanda, when she goes out to work, I am the one who stays with the children, I am the one who cooks her, I attend to them etc.

I told Ricardo it would happen the next day before Yolanda went out to work, to talk about it, and we stayed at a specific hour. The next day I arrived 2 hours before Yolanda left to work, and because I'm a friend of the two, she had no problem sitting with me to discuss the subject.

I told him that I was talking to Ricardo yesterday, and I told him everything we talked about, and that I'd like to know the version of events from her. Why had he had a drastic change in his home and in his way of being?

She very bitterly started by telling: You have been our friend since we were in school, you are one of the people who knows us the most, when Ricardo and I were a boyfriend, that is before we decide to live together the two, I got pregnant with him, I did not manage to go to university to stay and take care of my baby, Ricardo was a very conformist person , I always told Richard that he should try a little harder, to achieve better ambitions, to study or prepare professionally in some area, and that he did not plan to go and live with him, if I did not see him try any harder, because he preferred to stay like this, than to go and live with a very limited and unambitious man. He repeated to me on several occasions that what I needed was a greater motivation to achieve his goals. He assured me that, when I had a more serious responsibility, his effort would be greater.

Ricardo has the gift of conviction, so much of insisting on the final I agreed to his request. We both went to live together, in the first year we had our first child, then after 3 years was born the last, we have. Ricardo worked, but eventually, that is, that the income that entered the house was not consistent, often we find ourselves in difficulty paying the debts, and supplying at home. Then it was where I told Richard that if he had not yet found his motivation to be more ambitious inla Vida y no ser un conformist. **It was where he himself said, "If you know how to do it, then try it."**

She confessed to me that Richard's words had hurt her, I expected him to respond like a real man and put on his pants to improve our living condition, and she came out with that answer. It was where I decided never to rely on him, and to see how I got along with my children on my own. I called a friend I told her that I was interested in getting a job, no matter that, if she was a waitress, domestic worker whatever, since I couldn't demand much, I had no preparation, nor a college certificate for getting pregnant before time, I still get on with the idea of going back to college and overcoming myself, but that takes time and money , two things that have been missing at the moment. After a while my friend called me and informed me that she had got a job for me, but I didn't know if I was going to accept it; I told her I didn't care what kind of job it was, as long as it's legal she'd take it. My friend told me it was in a bar clubs serving drinks, I was excited about my first job I told her that I was fine, and that I accepted it. I started working the next day, at first, I didn't know anything, so it took me some time to adapt to the trade.

Yolanda started crying and telling me, there is no day when those guys don't touch me, I have to let myself caress and laugh, because if I don't I can lose my job, I have to sit with them to drink when they ask, and there are times when I can make some more money, it's my turn to be intimately with them.

She breathlessly expressed how disgusting she felt every time she got home, nor did her children want to hug so as not to get them dirty because of her conscience; everything Mommy had to do and endure for them, because the man in this house is not able to support a family. It's made me bitter my life, I've had to meet school friends in that bar, I've felt so Humiliated. That's why every time Richard wants to come and claim something, he insults him, he has no idea of the great hatred I have for him, for having me in this situation, he's a bit of a man.

When I looked at Richard, he also had tears in his eyes, and from there he realized wrong what he had caused, never again reproached Yolanda after that conversation. Fifteen days later she left work, because Ricardo this time worked greatly, and brought her talent to the sales area in a prestigious warehouse to this day. Now Yolanda manages to smile again and is happy with Richard's effort, they can now meet the needs, now with a third child on the way.

"A Person changes for two reasons: He learned too much or suffered enough."

CASE ANALYSIS #3

1. Locate the place where the problem originated.

A- Ricardo and Yolanda's problem began because of the need at home.

Tip: 90% of relationship problems always start from lack of communication or financial problems.

2. Determine what type of Communication was used before the Conflict?

A- On Yolanda's part an Open communication was used, verbally, very clear and direct to Richard.

Tip: Every woman should learn to take courage and not agree to live in mediocrity with her partner, because the man strives as far as the woman demands, if your demand is great then your partner's effort will be greater.

3. Analyze the first mistake made by one of the two.

A- The first mistake was made by Yolanda, knowing Richard's low-effort attitude and deciding to move in with him.

Tip: These types of mistakes are very common in couples, they join them, thinking that the character and attitude of the couple will change once they live together, but most of the time that does not happen, on the contrary, they become worse.

The key is to require the couple to change attitudes and fitness if they really want to take the relationship to the next level.

4. Define who lacked the Communication sent.

A- Ricardo failed to understand the importance of the message Yolanda wanted to convey to him at the time.

Tip: In the relationship, attention should always be paid to the request of the couples, as these can be a definitive message, of some decision that is to be made, and is only being waited for, the response or attitude of the couple once the message is sent.

5. Discuss what the couple tried to communicate to them at that time.

R- Yolanda I try to inform Richard that, if he does not strive to overcome himself, the relationship can fall into an emotional conflict.

Tip: Even conflicts within the relationship might be able to be avoided, if the receiver being communicated the message has enough capacity to understand, and even better understand what you are trying to say.

6. At what point the Tares was planted.

A- At the moment when Richard, for wanting to take the opposite of Yolanda when he demanded greater effort, his response caused Yolanda to enter the tares of mistrust, betrayal, selfishness and corruption.

Tip: He who does not restrain his tongue, what is indicated by a passage in the Bible: **"For all nature of beasts, and of birds, and of snakes, and of beings of**

the sea, is tamed and tamed by human nature; but no man can take his tongue, which is an evil that cannot be restrained, full of deadly poison. James 3: 7 and 8 (VRV).

He who masters his tongue can dominate his whole mind.

7. Which Pillar Element was affected and which tares was sown on the other side?

A- The element of Trust was greatly affected, where he brought with him his tares of mistrust, betrayal and selfishness, in Yolanda.

Tip: Each time an element of the pillar is affected, it will always be accompanied by its tares, the more tares it is sown the more difficult the restoration in the relationship.

8. What action or actions do you think bothered the other party?

R- Yolanda was annoyed by Richard's little effort and the response he gave her, which hurt her.

Tip: Nothing strikes harder than a word wrong or expressed by a loved one. Let's take care of our words, and we'll be taking care of our partner's heart!

9. Identify how many types of pillar elements have been affected and which types of tares have been sown in this conflict." Explain it."

A- The elements affected in this case were Communication, planning before deciding to live together, and Knowledge, sowing in relationship, deception, mistrust, corruption, and apathy.

Tip: All this was generated by a single word, a single expression at a bad time of discussion.

10. What was the real origin that caused the whole problem and how could it be avoided.? (Resolving this Question will be the primary key to avoid any Conflict in the future).

"The evil tree begins today from its root; so that tomorrow you don't have the misery to eat its fruits."

CHAPTER 8

#4 CASE

Raphael and Veronica

Losing to see the moon, to look at the shooting star.

"Weak Men have lovers, but strong men have family."

In a relationship it is important to value what we have, because it will be the only thing that will accompany us in difficult times.

On one occasion I had the opportunity to meet Rafael and Veronica, in a sports complex where some companies celebrated the end of the year festivities. I went with my family to be part of the event. Then the children went to play, and the mothers decided to go with them, and all the men stayed to chat, we talked about the different types of jobs we were doing. We shared data on the investments we had made, those that went well and the ones that went wrong, others talked about conquests and women. Among all the conversations one of them (Rafael) began to tell us a story that happened to him, and how he began to value his wife. He recounts that years ago, when he began his relationship with Veronica and decided to have children and live together, he and his family were one of the most exemplary before his friends, family and neighbors, in short, he was a family endowed with values, educated children, stable income and paid, the woman took care of the home and her children, he was safe, he was safe , providence and home protection. The perfect picture of a relationship.

Rafael confessed to us that he had a double life, because he had his family, but he also had a mistress named Lucia, a girl younger than him, tender and with an almost unexplored body, he told us that with her he went out everywhere, invented a night job to Veronica, so that he could stay with Lucia all night , they went out to dinner, to the cinemas and even on trips together, always with a good quarter for Veronica. He said that his wife never suspected anything, because he was a serious and respected man in his work, besides in his home there was nothing missing, and Veronica never had to work to help with household expenses.

Raphael recounts that while the woman was locked in her house, he had fun with Lucia, and gave her a gift that she never gave her wife, but she never denied Veronica money when she asked, for her to go shopping, go to the beauty salon, or for personal savings.

One day the company where he worked went bankrupt, Rafael and everyone else lost their jobs. He was worried at the time, it was the only income he had, because he hadn't had time to think about investing, for walking with Lucia.

He had one that other savings, but he knew that no income would soon run out. He decided not to tell Veronica at the moment so as not to worry her, but he did tell Lucia. Raphael's savings were gradually exhausted, because of the outings with Lucia, as he needed to keep Lucia happy and satisfied with him.

Veronica receives a call from the bank asking about Rafael, to catch up on his payment commitments, there were arrears in the letter of the department, as in his cards. She was surprised by that call. When she tried to call her husband's work to ask about Raphael, to inform him that the bank was calling, realizes that the company had ceased to exist already a few months ago.

Veronica, he annoys Raphael for hiding that information from him, waited for him to come back. When Raphael arrived, she acts as if she knows nothing about the closure of the company, and asked him how he had fared, he replies: a little exhausted, but well. She asks him to wash his hands and sits at the table to eat. And so, he did.

When they were eating, Veronica told him that the bank has 3 days locating it and has not been able to do so, did I ask them if they had a message to give you? they said to catch up on payment commitments, so you don't get overcharged, you're late in the apartment, the cards and the car. He tells her he was having trouble with his bank accounts, and he was already fixing that. She asked Rafael to tell her the truth of what was going on, because she had called to work and you know the company went bankrupt. Rafael doesn't have any other way than to tell her the whole truth about the company, so she asked him, and can you tell where you go all this time and you're late as if you were working? He told her that he was making some efforts to get another job and was late for her not to suspect or worry. She understood the situation, asked her that she had planned to continue the costs of the house and the payments of electricity and other things. He replied that he still had some savings while he managed to get a job. She didn't tell him anything anymore, she just said, "Don't worry we're going to get out of this."

But Rafael still insisted going out and spending the savings with Lucia, now the departures were less frequent with her and the gifts were scarce, when Lucia saw that Rafael was already without money, decided to tell him that he was no longer interested in continuing with him, because he did not meet his needs, and asked him not to return anymore. Raphael angry with Lucia and his attitude, had no choice but to leave and forget about it, and realize that it was only a financial instrument of Lucia.

Time passed and Rafael had run out of savings, due to his mismanagement, however, the bank stopped calling him, household expenses were always cancelled and Rafael knew it wasn't for him. He called Veronica and asked her how that had been possible, that no food was missing, nor the commitment to pay household expenses. Veronica replied: Remember you gave me for my personal expenses? He said yes, I remember it; Well, all these years I only took 10% of what you gave me and the rest I kept them in the bank for any time I really needed it. The emergency fund has not yet been necessary to touch them, and as long as you manage to get another job, I think we can live with what I have, at least 9 months, I don't think that in that time you haven't managed to get another job.

Raphael ended up saying that he had been surprised and remorseful, of having spent his money on Lucia for not giving the courage to the woman who was with him, for what he was and not by what he could give him. And you know it was the worst of it, after a while my wife confessed to me that she knew she had a mistress, because she once saw my shirt stained with lipstick, and she already looked at her once to tell her that her husband was with her.

He confessed to me that it was there, where he started asking me for an amount of money whenever he could, because he knew that sooner or later, my lover would leave me with nothing. She never claimed me, she never stopped taking care of me in the same way, she never changed, but I can imagine the great pain that put her through my selfishness.

Thank God I managed to get up again, because I'm lucky enough to have a woman like Veronica and now I try to give her priority to my wife, and I try to reward her in all these years that I did not attend to her.

"Friends must know, that women outside are with one for what you have, and not for who we are"

CASE ANALYSIS #4

1. Locate the place where the problem originated.

A- The problem originated in Raphael's heart

Tip: many times, the problems do not look for us, on the contrary, we look for the problem when everything is quiet.

2. Determine what type of Communication was used before the Conflict?

A- Referring to the moment, where Veronica discovers the truth of Raphael's dismissal, she tries to communicate with the Openly, verbally so that he would confess to her what was actually happening in the company and that he was doing all that time.

Tip: Lies always have short legs, sooner or later they will discover you in the lie.

3. Analyze the first mistake made by one of the two.

A- The only mistake was on Raphael's part, not to plan,

or organize his finances while he was in the days of fat cows.

Tip: It is important to know, that not all times are the same, there is time of abundance and time of scarcity, the difference is that initiative we take in a moment of abundance.

4. Define who lacked the Communication sent.

A- In the case narrated by Raphael we can say that the same circumstance was sending him discreet communications to himself and never understood him. For the way he spent his money, in the different ways that where his family didn't enjoy any of those moments with him, for walking from "Sugar Daddy"

Tip: Life often takes a toll on us through the mishandling of the goods God gives us in life to administer it in a way that is efficient.

5. Discuss what the couple tried to communicate to them at that time.

R- Veronica, I inform Rafael to be honest with her,

regarding her work.

Tip: In this case Veronica was an intelligent woman, who did not let circumstances sour her existence, despite knowing the truth in advance.

6. At what point the Tares was planted.

A- The tares wanted to be sown in Veronica's heart, but yet there was a tare of betrayal, selfishness, dishonesty, hypocrisy sown Raphael's heart.

Tip: if you look at a ship sailing over the sea, maybe one day you asked yourself the question like many How does something so heavy not sink?, the reason is that the boats do not sink by the water that surrounds it, but with the water that enters it. Don't let the circumstances around you sink you, I know how Veronica.

7. Which Pillar Element was affected and which tares was sown on the other side?

A- The element affected in this case was Trust, Transparency, Sincerity and Planning, in Raphael, in which he was sown the tares of deception, betrayal, selfishness, corruption, hypocrisy, dishonesty.

Tip: In life there are many people who have double lives, putting their interests above the family.

8. What action or actions do you think bothered the other party?

A- Veronica was annoyed by the fact that Rafael concealed that he was no longer working and made him believe that he was doing it.

Tip: Simply hiding a truth, of that magnitude, sends a negative message to the distrust partner.

9. Identify how many types of pillar elements have been affected and which types of tares have been sown in this conflict." Explain it."

A- The elements affected in this case, were 5, the Trust that brought with it tears of betrayal, Transparency brought deception and corruption, The Sincerity bringing dishonesty, and hypocrisy, Planning, bringing financial disorganization in Raphael that would later become a chaos, to pay off his debts.

Tip: It's amazing to see how people who don't need to enter into a family conflict can create an infinite world of trouble in themselves.

10. What was the real origin that caused the whole problem and how could it be avoided.? (Resolving this Question will be the primary key to avoid any Conflict in the future).

"The evil tree begins today from its root; so that tomorrow you don't have the misery to eat its fruits. "

CHAPTER 9
#5 CASE
REBEKAH AND WILLY

"Gifts and gifts"

"One of the most beautiful sensations a woman can receive is to know that they appreciate her."

Many times, we neglect the quality and virtues, which in love our partner, and believe that once we live under the same roof, and the qualities and attention should disappear.

"THE "UNSCUIDO" is the only one capable of killing the greatest love"

Willy has been married to Rebekah for several years, he works in a factory 30 minutes from home, and she in an office in the middle of the city only 10 minutes from home, the two are a young couple and still children, she is 28 years very attractive and he is 30 years old, he is also a handsome young man , that relationship they have born from college when they took the same career, Willy was a very detailed man with Rebekah, always surprised her with gifts and gifts when they were boyfriends. When they managed to live together, the two talked and decided that each would work, taking advantage of the that they did not yet have children, they could save enough for when the time presented and she had to stay at home, their payment commitments were minimal, the usual in each couple; light, telephone, cable, home, and car, power, fuel. He had his monthly expenses well planned and they sought to buy what was necessary, nothing ostentatious to have a healthy finance.

Suddenly Willy perceives that Rebekah from time to time, he brought to the house some new jewelry garments, which by his appearance he could see to be of great value, Designer bags, like shoes, before it was not very frequent, but when he observes that it was more often, he told her; why do you spend too much money on things you don't need at the moment, look you have a lot of shoes and bags that you've already bought, now spend on designer items, don't you think you're exaggerating and wasting money?, remember that we have a plan of expenses. She never answered anything and that even more bothered Willy.

A few months passed and Rebekah infrequently brought valuables, and never informed her partner, which resulted in she and Willy frequently entering into discussions, at Rebekah's insistence and her luxury items. Already their relationship was deteriorating with Rebekah's behavior.

When Willy turned to me for advice and told me about his situation with Rebekah, that's where he told me everything that was going on. I immediately told him to let me get home and talk to Rebekah too. We agreed to meet the next day in the afternoon, when the two were home.

When I arrived, Rebekah offered me something cold to drink, and that's when I told her, that Willy was worried about the relationship and told me what was going on, I asked Rebekah if she wanted to explain that behavior to me. She did not resist and agreed to say the following:

When Willy and I were boyfriends, he was very detailed with me, he always tried to surprise me with small details that for me were very great, because it was not about the value, but the action, the fact that he did that, made me feel very spoiled and at the same time special, those details were a very important factor that influenced our relationship for good. I know we plan to save, but I think the details at least once a month might appear.

Now I explain why I mention all this to you. It turns out that I haven't spent any dollars on these items, what happens is that in my work they started appearing on my desk from time to time, chocolates, sweets, other times flowers, and I didn't know how they got there, but I loved them, it was as if someone knew that those details filled me with satisfaction. Sometime later the person responsible for these gifts appeared, he was my boss; He told me that for him it will always be a gift, to see my face of joy when he found his gifts, and that the fact that not rejecting them encouraged him to continue to do so, was there that he started making me more expensive gifts, I actually wanted to stop him, but every detail of him always surpassed the last one. I never dared say anything to Willy, because I know that just accepting the gift from my boss was wrong. That's why I'd rather shut up and keep him thinking they were items I bought. My boss has always asked me out, but I've never done it, and yet he hasn't stopped filling me out with details. And today I needed to confess this to Willy, because I really know that I did not proceed well and our relationship has deteriorated by my behavior, and by silent ting this truth.

I asked Willy what he thought about it, he said, "It's true Rebekah that I haven't been detailed with you again, but I thought you understood why I stopped doing details to you, but today I realize that I could really lose you because of my carelessness, if you haven't accepted him an invitation to your boss, I thank you for being faithful to me , I promise I'll come back and do details, as I used to, I don't think I'll beat your boss with the ostentatiousness of his gifts, but I'll surely do them for love and without expecting anything in return."

Rebekah didn't leave her job, because Willy told her that she was very brave in saying it and believed in her integrity, all you have to do is keep accepting your boss's gifts, because no matter where you go, I can never be watching you for 24 hours, all I have to do is trust you, and your desire to take care of our relationship.

Today Willy and Rebekah, live more in love than before, she stopped the gifts to her boss, she didn't receive them anymore. Months later Rebekah decided to give up work to start at another who opened up more opportunities for her, and is pregnant with her first child.

"The integrity of a Woman is important, to nourish trust in the husband, and not to create negative thoughts about her"

The wise woman builds her house; plus, the fool with his hands knocks it down" Prov. 14:1

"A man must never lose the essence, with which he conquered his wife"

CASE ANALYSIS 5

1. Locate the place where the problem originated.

A- The problem stamped from Rebekah's work.

Tip: It is never good to accept gift from another person of the opposite sex, if it is not known what their intentions are, and if the intentions are more rightly suspected they should not be accepted.

2. Determine what type of Communication was used before the Conflict?

R- Willy communicated with Rebekah in an Open way verbally.

Tip: If you live with your partner and ask for an explanation of some anomaly that you are aware is happening, it is best to clarify your doubts, so as not to create imagination that will later create conflicts.

3. Analyze the first mistake made by one of the two.

A- The mistake that was made in the first instance was from Rebekah for accepting gifts from her boss.

Counseling or: I recommend not receiving a gift from another person, unless it is your birthday, or new year-end parties, or any holiday alluding to the date of the gift, if that is not the case, do not accept it from anyone, let alone if your partner does not know it. The fact that your partner stops giving you a gift does not give you a license to receive gifts or details from others.

4. Define who lacked the Communication sent.

A- The Young Rebekah, despite having understood the communication that Willy tried to convey to her, ignored.

Tip: Try to dodge the communication sent by your partner, thinking that in this way would not avoid a conflict, a mistake is made in doing so, since it gives way to the misunderstandings manifested in the mind of the couple. "He who shutss gives."

5. Discuss what the couple tried to communicate to them at that time.

A- Willy tried to communicate that they should follow the savings plan that the two had agreed.

Tip: Even though he was unaware of what was happening in Rebekah's work, she at least had to stop from that moment, receiving gift from her boss, because that gives the impression of being easy prey to the predator.

6. At what point the Tares was planted.

A- The tares were sown in Willy, seeing Rebekah ignore what he was telling her.

Tip: There is no worse discomfort in a relationship than being ignored or having your word and opinion as little matters. That is why you should attend to the opinion of the couple and value it as important as you would like yours to be valued.

7. Which Pillar Element was affected and which tares was sown on the other side?

A- The element of the pillar affected was Trust, and the tares of mistrust, betrayal and deception were sown.

Tip: To Willy ignore what was happening in his partner's work, he has no other way of thinking of Rebekah than she was not importing the pact he had done with Willy about saving for the future. That's what I believe in him all the tares that were sown, because of his partner, because she allowed him to leave the door open to the mind which is a workshop of the devil.

8. What action or actions do you think bothered the other party?

A- Willy is annoyed by Rebekah's attitude, of continuing to insist on buying valuables, not knowing what the reality of the facts was.

Tip: In the Bible there is a passage that fits like a ring to the finger to this case that says: "If food is to my brother the opportunity to fall, I will never eat meat, never to trip upon my brother" 1 Corinthian 8:13, in other words, if my attitudes or actions are going to cause a conflict in my relationship, the better not practical.

It rips the root of the bad tree today; and will not eat of its fruits tomorrow.

9. Identify how many types of pillar elements have been affected and which types of tares have been sown in this conflict." Explain it."

A- The elements of the Pillar of Finance concerned was communication, bringing with it the tares of mistrust, betrayal and deception.

Tip: A simple act can provoke, feelings of distrust in the couple, I was able to make you feel betrayed by some agreement you have made, and feel deceived by the lack of commitment on the part of the couple.

10. What was the real origin that caused the whole problem and how could it be avoided.? (Resolving this Question will be the primary key to avoid any Conflict in the future).

"The evil tree begins today from its root; so that tomorrow you don't have the misery to eat its fruits.".

CHAPTER 10

#6 CASE
DAVID AND PATRICIA

"A secret Discovered"

There is nothing hidden in life; that should not be manifested in its time."

"The house is wisely built, and with Prudence shall be Affirmed" Prov.24:3

Problems are faced with help when we recognize that they are stronger than us, wanting to be self-sufficient and showing that you have control over the situation, can sometimes become a lethal weapon or time bomb in the relationship.

Patricia came up to me one afternoon, to tell me what was happening at her house a few months ago. She was outraged at David, because she didn't know what was going on with him.

Patricia told me that she met David when he was with some friends at her work, as she was in charge of a mall, and one day David had an argument with a local employee. She very kind solved the misunderstanding. After that incident, David was impressed with Patricia, and every time he went to the mall, he tried to bring him a detail, until he managed to get him to accept an invitation to lunch. A few months later they started dating and later they were already living together, she tells me that everything was going very well in the first 14 months of their relationship, there was nothing missing at home, the payments were up to date, and she felt very comfortable with David. But after a while they started failing on punctual payments, and now they were behind in the monthly commitments, she didn't understand what was happening, to which she asked David to sit down and talk about it. He told Patricia that it was entirely his fault, as he had made an investment that went wrong and so far, he is working on it, but he neglects that everything will be all right, David told him. Patricia was a little calmer to hear David's answer, but when the end of the month came, the story of the bank call for outstanding payments was always repeated.

I tried to talk to David, but he now bothered if I made a comment about it, I don't know if he has a mistress because he's too late for the house, and smelling like cigarettes, because now it turns out he started smoking a while ago. And I'm thinking of getting away from him, now that I'm still on time.

I told her not to make hasty decisions, and to tell me when I could meet with the two of them, to know that she can tell us David, either at home or in my office, she asked me to spend the weekend at her house.

When the day came, we met, there were the two of us at that time. I asked Patricia to let David know what he was going to do if he didn't solve his problems today. She told him clearly that he could no longer be in that situation every month, and if he was being unfaithful to him to tell him at the time.

I asked David if he wanted to say anything that would change Patricia's mind. He then answered Yes! I want to save my relationship. He began by saying that he was very sorry for what happened, he apologized to his wife, having had to get to that point, to talk about his problem.

David recounts that it all started before I joined Patricia, the times I went to the mall to visit her, it wasn't exactly because I was going shopping, it's because I was visiting the casino that was inside the square, the day I argued with her worker, the reason was because I had lost my money and I was upset and I tried to de-like them with him , after I met Patricia I tried to get away from that, because she didn't know that part of me until today. Months ago, I met a friend, and he convinced me to come in for a while and I agreed. Wish! I would never have met him, and I regret not being stronger at the time, because now I have lost more than 75% of our savings in the casino, and I don't see the way to get it back, every time I go I feel like I'm going to get it back, but I'm sinking more into debt, to the point I took from our savings , and now we are in a very large debt because of me and my lack of control with this matter.

After he opened up to confess everything, things were easier to figure out, Patricia says she wants to help him and would be with him until she got over it. I recommended the number of a specialist who has been visiting them frequently.

I always have a habit of visiting couples who come to me for advice, the last time I saw them, I found that the relationship was already very strengthened. Patricia was already calmer to discover the truth for which she almost creates the separation in her relationship, and David for confessing her weakness for gambling, was more accessible to be able to receive help.

"Don't let a secret ruin your relationship, confess it and you'll be a good candidate to be forgiven"

"He that cover up his sins shall not prosper; but the one who confesses and turns away will attain mercy" Prov.28:13

CASE ANALYSIS #6

1. Locate the place where the problem originated.

A- The problem was already originating in David.

Tip: When we have an internal problem and we don't confess it to our partner, wanting to hide it will always make the relationship worse.

2. Determine what type of Communication was used before the Conflict?

A- Patricia used open communication, verbally with David to know what was happening.

Tip: You always have to value the couple when approaching responsibly and kindly looking for answers, that represents that if there is a question, then there is a concern.

3. Analyze the first mistake made by one of the two.

A- The mistake made was caused by David, by concealing his vice or weakness from gambling from his partner.

Tip: In problems between couples, you should always have the initiative to talk, remembering that for a relationship to be healthy and stable, you should never have a secret, because sooner or later these will be discovered and will be much worse.

4. Define who lacked the Communication sent.

R- David had trouble understanding or channeling Patricia's concern and concern when talking to him about what worried him.

Tip: Ignoring, the couple's restlessness, can aggravate the situation in the relationship, the healthiest thing is to sit down and talk to the truth, or simply eliminate the concern of the couple with a change of attitude.

5. Discuss what the couple tried to communicate to them at that time.

A- Patricia, I try to tell David, that she's too worried about the constant end-of-month situation and payment problems.

6. At what point the Tares was planted.

A- The tares were planted in Patricia at the time of seeing that every end of the month the same non-payment scenario was repeated.

Tip: We all have a sixth sense when we feel that something is not working well in the relationship, because each creates a pattern of behavior, that when changing it is easy to detect it.

7. Which Pillar Element was affected and which tares was sown on the other side?

A- The affected element was trust, bringing with its Patricia's distrust of David and a sense of betrayal.

Tip: When doubt and uncertainty enter into a relationship, it is normal to think the worst of the couple, because it has not been transparent, and has taken in little the honesty in the relationship.

8. What action or actions do you think bothered the other party?

A- Patricia was annoyed by the fact that David had

unusual behavior, and was unclear as to the reason for his attitude.

Tip: When we have a personal problem, the most practical thing is not to drag our loved ones with us, because they are not to blame for the bad decisions we make.

9. Identify how many types of pillar elements have been affected and which types of tares have been sown in this conflict." Explain it."

A- In this case several elements of the Pillar of Finance were affected in the relationship: Trust, which resulted in the tares of mistrust being sown, and betrayal in Patricia. David lost transparency and sincerity in the relationship, bringing with him deception, corruption and dishonesty.

Tip: There is no greater misfortune in a relationship than that of an uncontrollable vice, it is important that if you are going through something similar, try to get professional help or talk to your partner as soon as possible, the relationship is strengthened in overcoming each adversity, the greater the adversity overcome, the greater the basis in the relationship.

10. What was the real origin that caused the whole problem and how could it be avoided.? (Resolving this Question will be the primary key to avoid any Conflict in the future).

"The evil tree begins today from its root; so that tomorrow you don't have the misery to eat of its fruits"

CHAPTER 11

#7 CASE

EMILIO Y BRITANY

<u>"A dominant mind"</u>

"An egolatra person, will always boast, who is better than all, are people who hurt without feeling, regardless of humiliating loved ones even to their own family.".

Emilio and Britany, live on the north side of my city, in a middle-class area, according to what can be seen from the couple with the naked eye, are very normal like any other. But behind the door of the house, the reality that was hiding was different. He's a wealthy man, he met her when he worked in a designer clothing store, the first time he saw her, he was very much in love with her.

Britany didn't initially get her attention from Emilio, she said that every time he arrived, she did it in a prepotent way, believing he owned the world, and that's what Britany didn't like. He repeatedly tried to persuade her to leave, but she always rejected him.

One afternoon Emilio came to the premises, and approached him to ask him, what was the reason he always refused his invitation to leave, it was where Britany did not hesitate to tell him, that he was very prepotent and conceited, he did not like how he believed he owned the world for his money. And I don't like being with someone who looks over the shoulder of other people.

Emilio understood that, if he wanted to conquer Britany, he had to make some adjustments to his behaviors, after a few months Emilio had given his arm to twist, and always sought that Britany, understand that he has changed. After a while Emilio tried again and invited Britany out. This time she did not refuse the invitation. He took care of taking her to the best places in the country to impress her, and it turned out.

After going out with Britany for a few months, she asked her to quit her job and go live with her, she agreed to Emilio's request that she felt that, with him, she could get ahead.

After Britany decided to move in with Emilio, she used to stay home for 9 months while Emilio went out to see his business. Britany's family once came to visit her, because she had invited them, but she didn't say anything to Emilio. She prepared food for everyone and was congratulated for the new lifestyle she was living in. Then Emilio came and to his surprise the house was full of people that he had not invited, only greeted and went into the room, visually everyone realized that he was upset, and asked Britany if she considered that his attitude had been for them. She said No, she sure had a bad day.

When it was all over, and Britany's family came out, Emilio immediately called her and asked her what that daring meant, having brought strange people into her house, and apart from giving those people food, without him knowing anything. I didn't like that they sat in my room game imported from Italy, and Britany said to him: Wait a moment Emilio, the people who arrived, were no strangers, they were my family and I invited them because I wanted to be known, I never thought you'd go out with the rudeness of going to the room and locking you up, it was very bad of you. Emilio told Britany: I want you to have something very clear, remember that everything that is here, is mine, everything I bought with my money, or you forget that I brought you here, with nothing, even the clothes that you have on you I bought it myself, you have nothing here, for So, you can't be doing anything, without first informing me what you're going to do.

Britany hurt by his words, did nothing but accept with a head gesture. From then on, Britany knew what her position was in the house, and now she was insecure, of what she could and what she could not, in her own home, that situation led Britany to lower her self-esteem, she dared not leave Emilio's house, for fear of returning to her old life, and preferred to receive Emilio's humiliations and live luxuriously and show happiness only of appearance , you go back to running out of nothing and going back to your family's house.

"Dignity is a quality of very high value, which loses its essence when we trample it ourselves."

"People aren't poor because of the way they live, they're poor because of the way they think."

CASE ANALYSIS #7

1. Locate the place where the problem originated.

R- the problem originated in the heart, by Emilio's selfishness.

Tip: Often people show the true face of their heart when they have possessions or feel powerful, because a person does not change for what he has, but manifests what he really is.

2. Determine what type of Communication was used before the Conflict?

A- Emilio communicated to Britany verbally her way of thinking.

Tip: When a person begins to manifest his true Self, and makes you feel humiliated, it is the best time to think if you want to spend a whole life being humiliated.

No one has the right to belittle anyone, and no one has the duty to suffer such humiliation, if things did not work out as expected, then it is best to try again.

3. Analyze the first mistake made by one of the two.

A- The first mistake made in this relationship was Britany's, deciding to move in with Emilio out of interest and not love.

Tip: every time a relationship is united by interest, you will always find difficulties in the long life of it, so it is important to join a person who really values you as a person, for what you are and not for what you have or can offer.

4. Define who lacked the Communication sent.

R- Britany lacks to understand what Emilio wanted to tell him, because he was humiliating and decided to stay.

Tip: Don't let anyone trample you for material possessions, we have enough ability to reinvent ourselves, never allow yourself to become a prisoner of need.

5. Discuss what the couple tried to communicate to

them at that time.

A- Emilio, I'm trying to get Britany known: if you want to be here, you have to follow my rules.

Tip: One as a couple can tell you the things we like or don't like within the relationship, but we can never impose rules on them, because it would be a toxic relationship.

6. At what point the Tares was planted.

A- The tares were planted in Britany, from that humiliating conversation she had with Emilio.

Tip: Our words can carry bad seeds, take care of your words and take care of the heart of the one who hears you.

7. Which Pillar Element was affected and which tares was sown on the other side?

A- The affected element was communication, sowing in Britany feeling of mistrust, feeling betrayed by Emilio's conduct.

Tip: A man should treat a woman as a fragile glass, appreciate the effort that was taken to conquer her and not throw it away.

8. What action or actions do you think bothered the other party?

R- Britany was annoyed that Emilio, showed her true face that she had already known beforehand.

Tip: A person does not change attitude overnight, everything takes his process, he cannot pretend to deceive himself into believing that the changes are so easy and simple.

9. Identify how many types of pillar elements have been affected and which types of tares have been sown in this conflict." Explain it."

A- In the relationship two elements of the pillar were affected as they are, communication and knowledge, sowing with it the tares of mistrust, the feeling of betrayal, and the apathy of Emilio.

10. What was the real origin that caused the whole problem and how could it be avoided.? (Resolving this Question will be the primary key to avoid any Conflict in the future).

"The evil tree begins today from its root; so that tomorrow you don't have the misery to eat its fruits."

CHAPTER 12
#8 CASE
IVAN AND KEYLA
United by interest

"The Root of all evils, it is NOT precisely MONEY, but LOVE to MONEY."

"Some people will be loyal to your need for you. Once your needs change, so will you or loyalty."

While we know that money doesn't buy happiness, but it helps you largely in getting it, money no longer than you deny it is an essential factor in our daily lives, as 90% of our transactions in life are based on the use of money. If you're sick and need surgery, but it turns out the operation is too expensive, "Don't you think money could help you solve that? If your family is hungry or needs, wouldn't it do you any good to have money? Anyway, I could set thousands of examples so that we understand that money is not bad, it becomes bad, when your dependence is 100% on it, and you make it a god to You.

Even scripture says: I love you that you will be prospered in all things and have Health" ... 3 Jn 1:2. God is interested in your prosperity.

This is the case of Ivan and Keyla, they were a totally extraordinary couple, Keyla liked to be in the fashion trend, and he was interested to be updated with everything that was technology, the two enjoyed being traveling and living unique experiences, because Ivan's salary allowed him, he was very attentive to Keyla, made him gifts of all kinds, be it jewelry, designers in short, Ivan the times she could surprise her she did. I loved Keyla very much and so did she.

Iván was vice president of a prestigious multinational company, apart from his salary, it was up to him to receive the annual commissions, for the production of the company. The company where Ivan worked, he had to go through a financial crisis, and was forced to reduce staff in the company who accrued a high salary, so as not to go bankrupt and be able to withstand the current crisis. Undoubtedly, Ivan was one of the leading candidates in running out of jobs. But thanks to his capitalization, Ivan managed to save a good amount of money to cover his house expenses, and his banking responsibilities for a few months while he was in another job, or expect the same company to rehire him once he recovered from the crisis. A few months passed and Ivan neither called him the old company, nor did he manage to get a job, because of his position that demanded a lot of pay in his salary, that is why companies preferred to hire cheaper workmanships, and not hire him.

You don't have to be wise to know, "That every saving that doesn't earn income and only egress sooner or later will be scarce." That's what Ivan was about to experience with Keyla, and gifts, travel and shopping were over several months ago. Keyla was getting frustrated by the situation they were going through and saw no improvement in finance, because she didn't work, because she didn't need to, she just thought she'd have to work, she went into a depression, because she thought they'd say their friendships. It's not long before payment commitments came to be made up, and the complications of catching up on payments with banks started to aggravate the situation and put strain on the relationship. Keyla told Ivan that he gave him a month, so that his financial situation will be improved, but unfortunately it will be forced to abandon it and look for someone who can meet its expenses.

Ivan, was beginning to experience the stress of debt, a situation that I had never had the need to experience in self-meat. He told me that he never believed that he would have to go through need of that magnitude.

After a few months Ivan failed to get the job he wanted, so he was forced to take a job with a reduction of more than 60% of what he used to receive, and since he could no longer please Keyla's whims, he decided to abandon him. Ivan and Keyla's problem were not the magnitude of their debts, but the magnitude of their whims, because rich is not the one who has much, but he who needs the least." People in that social circle get used to it, just live in abundance, but they never learn to live in scarcity. If they learned to live with less, what he lacks today, tomorrow he would have plenty.

It is not the same to come with your partner from a level below zero (I mean capital), to find you at an overrated level, because when the riches start to be lacking, so love will begin to be lacking. Because always the interest was in possession, and never in the person.

"When you decide to join someone, make sure it's for you and not what you offer.

"Find someone who doesn't leave, when things get ugly.

CASE ANALYSIS #8

1. Locate the place where the problem originated.

A- The problem started when the shortage began.

Tip: In several relationships one of the most important factors that balance the relationship is finance, if you are not prepared for a financial shortage at any given time, a crack is created in the relationship.

2. Determine what type of Communication was used before the Conflict?

A- Keyla communicated in a verbal manner with Ivan.

3. Analyze the first mistake made by one of the two.

A- the first mistake was made by Ivan, for not planning on his expenses, nor organizing in making long-term investments.

4. Define who lacked the Communication sent.

R- Ivan lacks the communication That Keyla sent him.

Tip: a person who thinks about abandoning you when

things go wrong and you're still with that partner is definitely because he didn't understand that their relationship is just materially based and not on feelings. A person who loves will never think of turning his back on you at a difficult time.

5. Discuss what the couple tried to communicate to them at that time.

A- Keyla I try to inform Ivan that, if he did not improve his situation, he would unfortunately abandon him.

Tip: Every man likes to make his partner feel good, with travel and gift, but it is often good to get used to the basics, so that when there is a shortage, he only understands that it is temporary and not permanent.

6. At what point the Tares was planted.

A- The tares appear in Keyla's life the moment finance began to run low.

Tip: When you join a person, really see what underseals their relationship, whether they are sincere feelings or just material.

7. Which Pillar Element was affected and which tares was sown on the other side?

A- The element of pillar affected was trust, bringing a sense of betrayal and selfishness.

Tip: Such a statement, coming from the lips of the person who is supposed to be the first person to support you, it is normal that one cannot help but feel, distrust, and betrayal on his part.

8. What action or actions do you think bothered the other party?

A- In this scenario, Ivan was annoyed by Keyla's attitude, for not enduring difficult times.

Tip: When we are in a relationship and the difficult times come, it is best to be able to spend that situation with the couple, because every problem is temporary, but the experience lived will be permanent.

9. Identify how many types of pillar elements have been affected and which types of tares have been sown in this conflict." Explain it."

A- In this relationship, different elements of Pillar 2 of Finance had been affected in the relationship; first of all, the confidence, and planning, which brought with them tares, of mistrust, and disorganization, was affected.

Tip: When living in fat cow time it is a good time to be organizing your finances and preparing for the time of the skinny cows, which we all get at some point.

10. What was the real origin that caused the whole problem and how could it be avoided.? (Resolving this Question will be the primary key to avoid any Conflict in the future).

"The evil tree begins today from its root; so that tomorrow you will not have the misery to eat of its fruits."

CHAPTER 13
#9 CASE
MARLENIS AND CLAUDIO
A Self-Sufficient Woman

"One yourself is guilty of your disappointments, for creating such high expectations with such basic people."

Many times, we find women who have come through their own effort, and many of them think they are better off alone, then badly accompanied, but really the need to have someone by their side is stronger than the abstinence of being left alone. Nature shows that all living beings are designed to live in pairs, we see it in insects, animals, and humans, not only for the survival of species, but also for the survival of ourselves as people. This reality becomes difficult when it comes to knowing how to choose the ideal person you should be with, to lead a pleasant life. While it's true, "Things change over time and things change."

This is the case of Marlenis, a fighting woman who had come forward with her own effort, she had her own house, which she had built her way, has a very stable income, thanks to her having a prosperous business, has not made her a rich person, let alone a millionaire, but what generates her business leaves her to live a very comfortable life and without need.

Once, Marlenis became ill with a delivery man and had to replace him, and went to visit a client to deliver some orders from his company, but at that time she arrived the client was not there, and it was her turn to see her Claudio, a tall man, with a characteristic of playing sport and was good-looking, his education and way of treating Marlenis , left her sighing for him, (Marlenis, fell in love because she was younger than her and athlete's body) from that day she saw him, she tried to be the one who took the request exclusively to that client, with the intention of Having Asked her to return her.

After several months, Claudio noticed that Marlenis was interested in him, and it was where he decided to ask her out. In that invitation, Marlenis opened his heart and confessed to him how interested he was. Claudio very kindly expressed that he also had feelings for her, and if he liked it, he would like to continue dating her, to get to know each other better. (But in reality, Claudius saw an opportunity to conquer Marlenis, for being wealthy.) She agreed, and after a few months, they decided to go to live under the same roof, Marlenis insisted that the two live in the house, she told him that there, everything was already canceled and that they should only worry about the food and the basic expenses of the house, Claudio found the idea well and went to live with Marlenis.

Everything was going very well at the moment, Marlenis felt in good hands, and was still very much in love with him, it had been six months before living together with the two. A month later Claudio argues with the boss and quits his job, with the idea of staying at home living maintained by his wife. Marlenis told her not to rush to get a job, not to stress about it, when he wanted, he could go to get it, she said he could take care of the house expenses, while he solved his problem. Claudio thanked him for that. (Marlenis actually wanted Claudio to work, but at the same time he was afraid that he would get a mistress.)

About 3 months passed, and Claudio always asked Marlenis for money to go out to get a job, and she agreed, there were times when she told her that what she gave her was not enough, she also borrowed the car from Marlenis, and in passing used her debit card that Marlenis lent her.

Suddenly Marlenis noticed that a lot of money was coming out of his account and when he asked Claudio, he always told him that he used the money, to eat, or for fuel, etc. And she always believed him. (What really happened was that Claudius had a mistress and used Marlenis' money to take her for a walk, and to eat in her car.)

Marlenis, seeing that it was much more of the money out of his account, decided to take the card from Claudio and also the car, telling him that when he wanted to leave, he would warn him, that she offered to go with him, to make the necessary laps.

Claudius as he saw that things were going to get complicated with Marlenis, decided to end the relationship he had in hiding. Now Claudio did not go out looking for a job, he was only watching shows on the TV, and browsing social networks, he was very calm and comfortable where he was, there was nothing to worry, and as Marlenis told him not to stress about getting work, he took his words to the letter.

Marlenis came from work, and he always online or watching TV, Marlenis always watching the same picture, decided to talk to Claudio, and tell her that she believes it is time for him to look for a job to help her with household expenses.

Claudius replies; but you told me that when I felt ready for me to go out and get a job, and the truth still I don't feel like I'mlist, but I promise you next month, I'll go out and get a job. She nodded and told him it was okay.

When the month came, he actually went out to get a job, and after two weeks he managed to get one, but not with good pay, what he earned practically ran out, in paying his cards, and some commitments that he had made, could not help him to support at home. Marlenis was still taking on the main household expenses. Claudio didn't care much, because he knew Marlenis had to pay the expenses and with what he earned, he spent it for his own profits. Thus, began the couple's problems, Marlenis claimed Claudio for not cooperating at home and Claudio told her that she was a selfish woman, because she could well keep running the expenses, as if he were not there.

Then Marlenis understood, that Claudius was not going to change his perspective of the situation, because he preferred her to use his money, while what he earned would be used for his personal expenses. She understood that she had become ill accustomed to Claudio.

Marlenis did not want to demand much from Claudius, fearing that he would leave her again, although she found her shown that she was more interested in what she has and not what she is.

"Before deciding who to join, first know it more thoroughly, don't get carried away by its appearance, or its context and you will avoid days of bitterness."

CASE ANALYSIS #9

1. Locate where the problem originated.

A- The problem in this case originated in Marlenis, however bad to get Claudio to try no harder.

Tip: The fear of losing a person makes wrong decisions.

2. Determine what type of Communication was used before the Conflict?

R- Marlenis used, an open communication verbally to inform Claudio that it was time to get a job.

Tip: You should never take away a man's responsibility, it's a good to be able to help him at a time when the effort he makes doesn't work out, but helping him with the knowledge that doesn't make his best effort to overcome his problems is wrong to get used to.

3. Analyze the first mistake made by one of the two.

A- The mistake was made by Marlenis, in enduring

Claudio's uncommitted attitude in helping her with the expenses of the house.

Tip: Everyone who has a good flow of money, and manages to get a younger partner, 90% of the cases is because he is behind his money and not out of feeling, most of the time the money he gives that person is spent on another hidden relationship he has.

4. Define who lacked the Communication sent.

R- Claudio lacked the understanding that Marlenis was uncomfortable with his attitude mattered little with the basic expenses of the house.

Tip: When you get used to a person and then want to try to change them, it will be too late.

5. Discuss what the couple tried to communicate to them at that time.

R- Claudio hinted at Marlenis, accept me as I am or leave me.

Tip: Literally Claudio hinted that he was willing to stay with her, if he did not harass him with the expenses of the house. When you focus on such a situation, don't be afraid to be left alone, it's better than being mis accompanied.

6. At what point the Tares was planted.

A- It was sown at the time Claudius learned that Marlenis showed interest in him.

Tip: When you show a lot of interest in a person, most of the time they will use that feeling to take advantage. That's why I recommend you never be the hunter, but the prey so you can spark a real interest in someone.

7. Which Pillar Element was affected and which tares was sown on the other side?

A- Trust was one of the elements affected in this situation, bringing with it a situation of mistrust.

Tip: You surely managed to hear that, "Not all that shines is gold," for believe it is so.

8. What action or actions do you think bothered the

other party?

R- Marlenis was annoyed to recognize that Claudius was not with her out of feeling, but out of interest.

Tip: It's never good to show people what you have, because then they focus on the material and not the sentimental.

9. Identify how many types of pillar elements have been affected and which types of tares have been sown in this conflict." Explain it."

A- On this occasion two elements were affected, the trust that sowed distrust as we had mentioned, and the knowledge on the part of Claudius that sowed apathy in him.

Tip: Don't enslave a person who is only with you so you can offer them, value yourself and decide to seek your happiness next to someone who really feels the need for you.

10. What was the real origin that caused the whole problem and how could it be avoided.? (Resolving this

Question will be the primary key to avoid any Conflict in the future).

"The evil tree begins today from its root; so that tomorrow you don't have the misery to eat its fruits."

CHAPTER 14
#10 CASE
ISABEL AND PETER

A help that brings more trouble

It is very good to have a couple that serves as your ideal help, because for that it was created by God, but often the best help that can be offered to a person is not to try to help them.

Without a doubt we are all exposed to be helped at any given time, and only pride would be able not to accept help, it is always necessary to receive it either physically, spiritually or economically, no one is exempt from the need for help.

This is the case of Isabel and Peter, two couples with more than 5 years of being married, Peter has always considered that he should take responsibility for the expenses in the house, Isabel always takes care of her and take care of the two children who have, she actually made it very heavy to attend to her home as any housewife (Taking care of the house is the most complete and exhausted work that may exist to this day, you do not rest is a 24 hour job, You have to be a teacher, nurse, cook etc.) cleaning, washing and more. He had always wanted to go to work to forget about the trades of the house and hire an employee. Peter works independently in a mechanics workshop, is an entrepreneur and decided to set up his own workshop, his income depends on the repairs that he manages to make and deliver in his time, not always the months are good, there are times when income rises and other times when they go down, (all of which start a business knows that good seasons and bad seasons must come, you just have to be prepared for the bad seasons). Peter knew that perfectly, but with years of experience he had managed to understand his good and bad seasons, so it didn't cause him much stress those moments, he tried not to go into debt so as not to have unnecessary money outings. He managed to adapt according to the situation presented to him, Peter's business allowed him to meet the payment of basic services, food and mortgage, also gave his wife to attend to the beauty salon and to move from time to time to buy dress for herself and the children.

At a time when the season was going down, Isabel, seeing her husband working and he was just carrying the burden of the house, saw a great opportunity to propose to Peter that she would allow her to get a job and help her in the expenses of the home. Peter was not very convinced, because it was more important for him that the mother took care of her children, and she gave her the values and help them in her studies, plus the children were very young, the eldest was 5 years old and the baby was only a year old. She explained the plan she had if she could work. Peter asked her how she would cover her position in the house and how she could help him with the expenses.

Isabel told her that she could cope with 50% of the mortgage payment, take on her own expenses at the beauty salon and with buying dresses for her and the children and he would only worry about canceling the other 50% of the mortgage and basic services, food, and tuition.

Peter asked Elizabeth that, if she was sure of everything she was saying, because some things are the other plans is to carry it out as one imagines it, very sure of herself she replied thatis. Peter asks him and who will attend the house, and the children? Isabel told him that he also had a heavy hire employee.

Peter did not agree with Isabel, but in order not to limit her in his wishes, he agreed to make it very clear to him, that he was grateful for the initiative she had had to help him, that in these 5 years he had been able to carry the burden alone and did not weigh on it to continue to do so, but that he would be clear that if it did not work and things did not go as she expected then that he would voluntarily give up the idea.

She accepted the condition he put on her, went out to have several resumes and within a month she was called in for an interview and they accepted her. Isabel started working and hired an employee first to help her at home.

When her first fortnight arrived, Isabel only caught up with her to pay the mortgage as she had left with Peter, and cancel the employee, because the workshop was still in low seasons. Peter smiled told her very well, congratulated her and she was very happy to be able to help Peter and remained motivated. After he had spent two months at the job Isabel had obtained, he applied for a loan from a person who dedicated himself to offering money to colleagues at 20% interest, because it could not accommodate him for the beauty salon, nor for the other expenses. Everything was invested in the mortgage and the employee's payment.

Then Isabel got credit card offers, the year of working at the company, applied to two banks and they were handed over. She didn't comment on Peter, because she knew he hated debt, but she thought she could keep control of them to help with expenses and because she wanted to take the kids shopping and have fun. Now when the fortnight came, Isabel had not only to cancel the mortgage, but to the employee and the lender, she was already in a financial collapse, only working to cancel debts and not dared to tell Peter that he was sinking into debt, and that they were growing more and more.

One afternoon Isabel receives a letter from the company, where she was thanked for her services rendered, and the completion of the contract.

Now Isabel was in great trouble, the liquidation that was due to her, was not enough to cancel the lender, but only the interest, she would only be enough to pay her share of the mortgage and only half to the employee. She had no other way to tell Peter what was going on, she was very sad and crying because she felt that instead of helping what she did was to create one more debt to Peter.

For a moment Peter was upset with Isabel, having asked for a loan without having notified her, and now he had to assume it, already the workshop was beginning to return to his production levels, but still could not cancel that debt, he could only cancel the interest while the workshop could pay off that commitment. Peter told Isabel that they would have to carry that debt for a few months, because the money he managed to generate had always been budgeted for household expenses and their commitments.

Ten months passed by paying interest, before they could cancel the loan he had applied for at the company, they asked the lender to freeze the interest so that he could pay the capital and he accepted. Anyway, she'd already made a lot of money in interest and was a former partner. Now Isabel's cards needed to be cancelled, she could only afford the minimum payments.

Now Peter's income was not enough to pay for the debts acquired by Elizabeth, nor the commitments she already had, it had to always be decided that it should be paid and that it should not, they were now immersed in a debt that they could not cancel, to which it led Peter to enter the stress and discussions with Elizabeth, because of his negligence and irresponsibility that brought them all that debt chain. Banks kept calling about their money, and the relationship between the two began to deteriorate because debts were growing more, and Peter now could not afford to have bad seasons.

"There are times when the best help we can offer others is not to help them, because by a good deed we want to do we can turn it into a sea of problems that didn't exist before"

"If you go through a bad time, keep walking the bad is the time, not you."

CASE ANALYSIS #10

1. Locate the place where the problem originated.

A- The problem started with Isabel's idea of wanting to go to work, with the purpose of avoiding chores at home.

Tip: It is true that there is no more complete and more exhausting work than that of a housewife. But it's also the only one that gives you the privilege of being with your children and creating good values for them.

2. Determine what type of Communication was used before the Conflict?

R- Peter used open and verbal communication with Isabel.

Tip: If your partner feels he can with the burden even in difficult times, the best help you can offer, is careful attention, words of encouragement and let him know how proud you are of him. That will motivate man to reinvent himself more and more every day.

3. Analyze the first mistake made by one of the two.

A- The mistake was made by Elizabeth in wanting to escape the responsibility of the home.

Tip: What others wish to be able to do, there are those who despise it. Many people would like to stay home caring for their children. He values the freedom he has, because they are hardly repeated twice.

4. Define who lacked the Communication sent.

A- Isabel, because she's focused on supplant, she lacks to understand what Peter was trying to communicate to her.

5. Discuss what the couple tried to communicate to them at that time.

A- That it was not necessary for her to worry about getting a job, which for him was the most important was the care and education of her children with a maternal figure.

Tip: It is true that there may be sexist men who do not like their wife to work out of insecurity, thinking that he will get a lover or for fear of his independence from him, but in many cases the man with good thought prefers that his children be in the care of his mother.

6. At what point the Tares was planted.

A- The moment Isabel got a job.

Tip: There are jobs that, instead of becoming a Blessing, becomes doom.

Seek to put before God all your plans so that He may bless your way.

7. Which Pillar Element was affected and which tares was sown on the other side?

A- Planning was the affected element in Elizabeth's decision, which was sown the tares of disorganization in Elizabeth's life.

8. What action or actions do you think bothered the other party?

R- Peter was annoyed by the fact that Isabel had been indebted to that magnitude not only with lenders, but with the banks.

Tip: He who is able to understand that life without debt is lived better, will never fall into the anxiety of acquiring material things in advance, but will know how to wait and understand that everything has his time and good things come to the one who knows how to wait.

9. Identify how many types of pillar elements have been affected and which types of tares have been sown in this conflict." Explain it."

A- The elements affected in this relationship were Planning on The Part of Elizabeth, and knowledge, which brought with them a disorganization in finance within the relationship, by the misinformation that was sown in Elizabeth, when acquiring the debts.

10. What was the real origin that caused the whole problem and how could it be avoided.? (Resolving this

Question will be the primary key to avoid any Conflict in the future).

"The evil tree begins today from its root; so that tomorrow you don't have the misery to eat its fruits."

CHAPTER 15
SOURCE OF THE PROBLEM

In this chapter, we will answer question 10 of our questionnaire of each case, so that they can compare yours with this book, the conclusions of the other 9 questions are for a personal criterion analysis, in any case if you want to know more you can write to my blog, or to the email that is in the final part of the book.

#1 CASE

Diana and Fernando: First of all, the problem originated in Fernando, because he was unclear about the role of men and women in the home. **(If a man does not believe to bear full responsibility for a home, then it is better not to think about having one until he feels responsible enough, so as not to force his wife to take his place.)**

#2 CASE:

Francisco and Paula: in this case the problem originates in Francisco, for neglecting the need of the couple and giving Paula a bad answer when she asked for money the first time to fix himself.

(The woman is like a flower in a garden, the more the

more beautiful the care she gets.)

#3 CASE

Ricardo and Yolanda: The problem starts with Ricardo, by leaving no more options for Yolanda, for not ambition more in life, and by having a proactive woman, it is normal for her to seek her own survival for her own.

(If you want a woman to be an angel, then put the heaven down.)

#4 CASE

Raphael and Veronica: The biggest mistake man often makes is spending on women, which he doesn't spend with his.

(Life has its own KARMA, corrects what is wrong, and gives us a good lesson that helps us appreciate what we despise.)

#5 CASE

Willy and Rebekah: Start with Willy, by trying harder to save and stop filling her partner with detail, to the slightest that it seems that gesture makes a woman feel appreciated. **(A detail will always come to us in a moment and cannot be rejected, depending on the way and purpose offered, most of the time they are offered supposedly without wishing for anything in return, or out of gratitude. Both man and woman should be aware of giving gifts and details to their partner.)**

#6 CASE

David and Patricia: Clearly the problem stems from David's hidden vice. **(Vices, not only limited to the casino, but to alcohol, drugs, women, it is important to overcome vices to sustain a Healthy and Stable Financial Pillar.)**

#7 CASE

Britany and Emilio: The problem was caused by Britany herself, by **dears** carry for the pleasures that Emilio offered him and not by his instinct that was already notorious in Emilio that was dominant. **(It is important to give more time to unmask the true Self in People.)**

#8 CASE

Ivan and Keyla: The origin of everything, was Keyla's for loving money more than her partner. **(The root of all evil is not money, but love of money.)**

#9 CASE

Marlenis and Claudius: The problem originated in Marlenis, for not generating pressure on Claudio, and letting Claudio's appearance and youth influence. **(Don't look at the beautiful, or the height of his opinion, because surely, it's just appearance and no feelings.)**

#10 CASE

Isabel and Peter: The problem originated in Isabel, by trying to flee chores at home, and to acquire debts without having a permanent job. **(There is a time in life where we want to help in the relationship, but it doesn't always come out as you expect, and we are hurting you more.)**

CHAPTER 16
INDEBTEDNESS PATTERNS

It's important to know that all banks need to borrow people so they can have control over them. Acquiring a debt is always started by the same set of patterns in people with little knowledge in finance.

First, we are always happy with what we earn and manage according to our income.

Then we ourselves created a need, which never really was until we saw our friends, companion or family have it.

We start with the credits, because we think they're a fine print and we'll have no trouble paying.

Then there comes a real need that we do not overlook, and by using our resource to meet the needs that we create ourselves, we have no room to face which is really a necessity.

That's where we see it more feasible to ask for a bigger loan, not knowing how we're going to cancel it, but we think the first thing is to solve and then think how we cancel.

CAPITULO 17
FINANCE COSEJOS IN THE RELATIONSHIP

Don't buy anything you don't need. (Before I buy anything, I've learned to do it with a cold head, rock if I really need it or it's just for emotion and then I decide.)

Don't invest in business you don't know. (Investing in a business, where you have no idea of anything, is like trying to get into the pool without knowing how to swim)

Always let your partner know if you plan to get into a debt. (communication before debt is the best thing in the couple, because if something unforeseen happens the two can face it together without blaming anyone.)

Try not to buy anything on credit. (There is a saying that says, that to get something you have to go into debt, I think otherwise, but I can pay it then I pass it, or saving to acquire it, because equally the credit you would have to pay it multiplied by three).

Get away from credit cards. (they are a solution today, but a problem tomorrow.)

If you're going to get a debt, make it a good one. (There are good debts and bad debts, the good ones are the ones you'll use to put money in your pocket and with yourself to write off the debt. (Example: Investment) and bad debts, are the ones that will take money out of your pocket, and in the end, you must cancel it with your own money. (Example: Remodeling, purchase of sound equipment, travel, vacation etc.)

Don't buy everything that comes out online. (Online shopping becomes a vice, as you don't use cash, using the card becomes easier, and you don't feel the expense, until the end of the month when the bills arrive.)

Don't buy everything that's on the TV. (Ads are designed to convince people using neuromarketing) that is, they deceive your mind.)

CONCLUSIÓN

If we can see in all the stories, the total responsibility of finance in the relationship lies with Man. Women have the option to work and help with expenses, but it is not their obligation as long as they live with a responsible man.

I advise women, before we go to live with a man, remember that we all show our best image, we become politicians promising, and in the same way lacking in promises. Not only look at your appearance, but your goals and ambitions, get to know it thoroughly, ask him and above all make sure he's already working. (Remember that it is not only love that is lived)."

I advise men to take care of the woman who decided to go and live under the same roof, because in doing so, they are betting everything on you. Don't take her so you can treat her as an employee, but as a more fragile glass. Make sure your seeds are the best in their garden and it will bear the fruits that you expect.1 PETER 3:7

"If thy seeds are Good, then their fruits will be good too"

Epilogue

Everything we must understand that if you get along with Finance, we will enjoy a good healthy and stable relationship Healthy and Stable.

Be disciplined and save days of bitterness and stress.

Thanks

To thank God, first of all, who gave me the experience and ability to write this book, to help men and women do their marital duty.

www.ingramcontent.com/pod-product-compliance
Lightning Source LLC
Chambersburg PA
CBHW021404210526
45463CB00001B/211